The Golden Keys for Outstanding Customer Service Experience

Teddy Kelemwork

DEDICATION

I dedicate this book to my wife, Biruktait, a

customer service industry professional over a

decade. You are a huge part of my success

and I love you.

The best part of your life is ahead of you, and

together we are the authorized distributors of

God's resources.

-Teddy Kelemwork

PREFACE

Suppose you are asked to write a preface of a book. What do you write about?

- ✓ About the subject of the book?

- ✓ About your philosophy of the subject?

- ✓ About the author?

All of the above are viable options as the subject of a preface. I wrote about the author. Why? The subject of customer experience is of existential importance to every organization regardless of the mission. No organization exists without customers and without satisfied and repeat customers. I believe it will help the readers to know the character and the essence of the author and the source of the message. Who is Teddy, the author? Having known and having worked with Teddy for the last 10 years, I sum up my understanding of Teddy in 3 key words that will interest the readers- (1) Smile (2) Excellence (3) Dreams.

Smile: There is always a smile on Teddy's face regardless of life challenges he may be experiencing. I know a smile is contagious and a good thing. I am certain he wrote this book while smiling. I hope you feel Teddy's smile while reading this book.

Excellence: Teddy is a man of excellence. He conducted several customer service training sessions for my clients and spoke at several events I hosted. During all of these opportunities, Teddy has been memorable and left an excellent impression of excellence on the audience. I am certain, Teddy wrote this book with the spirit of experience, and you will be experiencing excellence while reading this book.

Dreams: Teddy is a man of big dreams. When you are around people of big dreams, you catch on the dreams and benefit from them. When Teddy and I first met, he was sharing with me his dreams of collaborating to establish global industry-recognized training programs. Many years after Teddy invoked these dreams, I am now vigorously engaged in making Teddy's dreams of making this a reality. I am certain you will catch on some of Teddy's dreams of achieving greatness. Without doubt, my life has been transformed because of being affiliated with and being a friend of Teddy.

I encourage you to expect to be transformed while reading Teddy's book on customer experience.

Make it a fantastic day!

Gabe Hamda, PhD, SPHR

www.icatt.net

PERSONAL MOTIVATION

It was near Washington Dulles Airport at lunchtime. I was hungry and needed to grab something to eat. I found a local sandwich spot attached to Sunoco gas station. I walked in and stood in line, contemplating what I wanted to eat. My turn came and I stated, "I would like to have a 6-inch wheat bread with turkey and cheese toasted please." I pulled out my wallet to pay. Then I heard the person handling cash say, "Only cash- we don't take cards." I checked my pocket to see if I had any cash, and I did not. Thus, I told the person fixing my sandwich, "Well, why don't you take the card number and run it manually, because

I don't have cash". She stated, "It's not up to me- the machine does not work." I also looked to the cashier and she responded saying, "I could not do that as the device does not work now." I recognized this is where the blaming game begins, and no one wants to take ownership to facilitate a positive outcome. Can you imagine how I felt? I was hungry, my sandwich was just moments away from being devoured, and my mouth was continually watering, unfortunately, no one wanted to extend a solution in this situation to help me out. It was disappointing. Even though I was willing to share my credit card information, to offer a solution of running it manually later (when the machine would be activated), they simply, void of empathy, declined. I determined at that moment that would be my last visit to this venue. The incident dug deep into my memory and suddenly sprung up when I was looking up to purchase a new TV. It was the month of November and we sought to purchase a new one from Best Buy. We were delighted to see it was priced almost 50% less than the Original price. We were pleased to acquire this high definition 65-inch screen at an affordable rate. We thought, hey, you cannot get wrong with that. However, to our dismay at the six months mark, the TV malfunctioned. We were just beginning to enjoy it! Oh, my! I'm hesitant about Purchasing extended warranty offers and had refused it here. To make matters worse, living through a pandemic, we were quarantined; all the whole family could do was stare at each other without our brand-new TV. What are we going to do?

I desperately checked if it was still under warranty. I called up the manufacture and shared with them the negative experience we had. They asked me to take a picture of the serial number and the screen and asked me a few questions. With an apology, they asked me to email them the picture and the serial number and said they would either send a technician or replace the TV. On inquiring how long it would take for them to make things right, they said it typically takes 4 to 6 weeks. However, if I make a special request and mentioning our situation that we're sitting at home without a TV, they told me they'll do their best. It was their opportunity to redeem and restore confidence to their customer in the product and service they can deliver. Standing true to their promise, in 14 days, they sent me a check with no further questions asked. From their customer service via phone to the entire process, I found they issued a sincere apology and sought to make the wrong right! That's what I call restoring confidence! I was impressed with their utmost professionalism.

I thought about the two disparate experiences I acquired as a customer, and decided to pen down my thoughts and feelings in the form of this book- "The Golden Keys for Outstanding Customer Service Experience." Hope you enjoy reading the book and benefit from it.

Acknowledgement

I want to thank my cheerleader Dr. Jerusalem Merkebu (PhD), Assistant Professor HJF for the Advancement of Military Medicine, and my mentor Dr.Gabe Hamda(PhD, SPHR), CEO of Icatt Consulting, for their ongoing support and professional guidance throughout my life and in this project. Without them it wouldn't have been possible to complete this project.

I want to thank my research assistant Dr.Konica Paul Chakraborty (PhD) for her hard work and supporting me write this book. She deserves a big thank you for all her efforts in collating information, analyzing and polishing up the final work.

TABLE OF CONTENTS

INTRODUCTION

> *"Excellent customer service is the number one job in any company! It is the personality of the company and the reason customers come back. Without customers, there is no company!"*
>
> **-Connie Elder**

Customer service is the bloodline of every organization- Connie Elder directly hits this target as every business organization's success or failure depends on its flow of customer service. In any business organisation, while serving the customers, one should be able to consider one's identity beyond the single department he or she is serving at. Instead, the focus of thought should rest on the larger life of the organization. Absent such a focus, the organization would cease to grow beyond its ability to deliver engaging customer service.

Heeding the wisdom of the proverb- **Life and death are in the power of the tongue,** it would be correct to say that, the life and death of an organization depend greatly upon the quality of service delivered to its customers. Therefore, to ensure the long and healthy life of any and every organization, it is very important to set the goals of customer service higher, to take it to the next level. This is where one needs to visit the needs of a customer from an ACRONYM viewpoint and focus on **consumer experiences.**

- C – COMMUNICATION
- U- UNDERSTANDING
- S- SERVITUDE
- T- TOLERANCE
- O- OWNERSHIP
- M- MANAGEMENT
- E- EXPERIENCE
- R- RESTORATION

People will forget what you said. They will forget what you did. But they will never forget how you made them feel.

Maya Angelou

With customer experience, the words of Maya Angelou strike out as real truth. Customers will only remember how the service representatives of a business made them feel, and hold on to a long-standing emotion arising out of that feeling while everything else will wear off and fade away. Only their experiential memory of the moments of interactions and the associated feelings and emotions would stay.

1. Can you think for a minute about an outstanding customer service experience you have had?

2. What made you remember that experience?

3. Was it of purchasing the product or the service encounter that made you feel that way?

Everything ultimately boils down to how the customers were made to feel while they were being served. The difference between an outstanding customer service experience and a mediocre one is the impression that stays on a customer's mind. Sometimes it might be even difficult for a customer to explicate the experience with words.... though the feelings stay engraved in the memory for a long time, often forever.... which frequently serve as 'word of mouth'-negative or positive.

However, one thing everyone can assert with confidence is that they had received royal treatment that made them feel special.... which converts to confidence in the organization that made them feel special. Let us explore in brief, the periphery of the acronym CUSTOMER in the chapters that follow.

1

COMMUNICATION: THE ART & HEART OF CUSTOMER SERVICE EXPERIENCE

"Communication is the glue that keeps customer experiences from falling apart."

-Adam Toporek
Customer Experience Strategist

Communication is an essential tool for building relationships and is an art. It lies at the core of every organization's effort to build a relationship within itself, with the external sponsors or stakeholders, and with the customers who are its spinal cord. Being vital to consumer experience, whether physical or virtual, communication has many stratums involved even in non-communication centric activities like placing online orders for products or services to checking out from that platform. It's a continuous process while creating customer experience, starting right from the stage of generating or gathering market information through the website language to personal communication through emails or other digital or non-digital platforms or during automated experiences.

While communicating, we use both verbal and nonverbal communication. Different types of verbal communication are used to suit different communication objectives, where the choice of words, the display of body language, the tone and pitch of the voice, the pause and modulations, using images and illustrations...each play a very dominant role in creating customer experience through communication.

Let's check out the role of communication in this scenario.

Case Study: Hewlett Packard, the multinational IT Giant

The major ways companies can increase their revenue is by increasing and retaining customer loyalty. Customers are more sensitive to the quality of goods and services delivered to them than the price of it; hence companies are more concerned about customer satisfaction despite the size of their market share. They look for new ways to meet customer expectations, striving to satisfy them more. From conducting market research to getting feedback from them on products and services, companies would do all it takes to address and adapt to the needs of their customers.

The International Business and Economics Faculty of The Bucharest Academy of Economic Studies in Romania carried out a case study on the contract administration department of a multinational IT company that provided services to several countries namely- Belgium, France, Luxembourg, Germany, Italy and UK for companies namely-

Oracle, Orange, Samsung, Nokia, Philips, Hewlett Packard, Petrom, and Rompetrol. Here the case study of only *Hewlett Packard* would be discussed as it holds on to the rank of 109 in the list of Fortune 500 companies from 2011 till 2020.

Hewlett Packard (HP) first written by co-founders Bill Hewlett and Dave Packard since 1957 were guided by Dave Packard's words, that- "People have to work together to achieve common objectives and to avoid working in different directions if it has to achieve the highest level of efficiency and success."

The company's main objectives include – profit making, achieving market leadership, generating development, acquiring management capacity, bearing international presence. However, the most important objectives are retaining customer loyalty and employee engagement. HP believes that to retain their customers, it is essential to listen carefully to them and understand their true needs, and then provide them with solutions that will get reflected in their success. Competitive total cost of ownership, quality and inventiveness, and the way of doing business determines customer loyalty.

Participant countries in the study: *Belgium, France, Luxembourg, Germany, Italy, UK.*

The study aimed to reveal, how designing and implementing a *new communication strategy* in relation to the customers helped the company overcome communication barriers and increase customer satisfaction and loyalty. The company being aware of the risk of customer dissatisfaction, came up with the concept of CRM or Customer Relationship Management, and met their customers in two phases through an online study in September 2011 and in March 2012 where the customers were asked to answer a set of questions when they accessed the company's website, aimed to measure these aspects –

→ overall customer satisfaction
→ ease of contact
→ responsiveness and ownership
→ professionalism and knowledge
→ advance notification
→ time to review

→ accuracy

→ ease of understanding

→ turnaround time for request

→ online satisfaction

Customers expressed their opinions as follows:

- very satisfied ⎤
- satisfied ⎦ — Top of the scale

- dissatisfied ⎤
- very dissatisfied ⎦ — Bottom of the scale

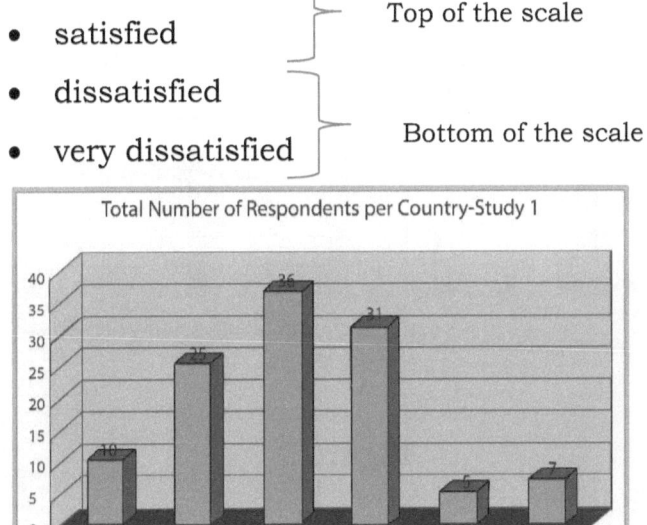

Figure 1

Figure 1 shows the number of respondents in each of the six participating countries in the study in phase 1, and brings out the following results.

41% of the interviewed clients were satisfied or very satisfied with the department generally and 23% of the respondents said they were dissatisfied or very dissatisfied.

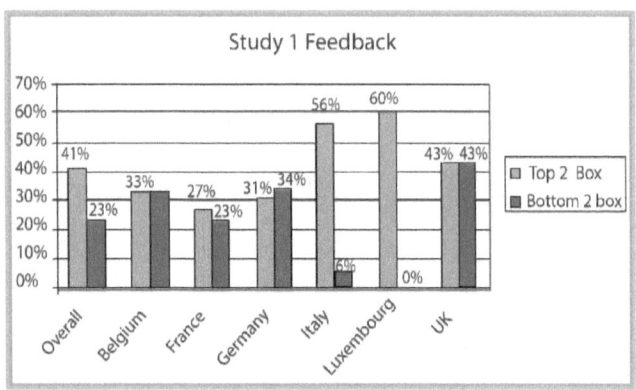

Figure 2

Figure 2 represents 33% of the Belgian customers responding within the top of the scale, while an equal percentage recorded their response for the bottom of the scale.

French customers said they were rather satisfied than dissatisfied. 27% of their responses were within the upper part of the scale, while 23% on the lower part of the scale. For Germany, 31% of responses were recorded within the first category of the top of the scale and only 34% in the second category of the top of the scale. For Italy and Luxembourg, majority of responses were positive, 56% of the Italian responses were in the top of the scale and only 6% on the lower part; and 60% of the responses from Luxembourg were at the top of the scale and surprisingly there was no response at the bottom of the scale. For the UK, the same percentage of 43% was recorded in both parts of the scale.

Steps taken: HP studied the positive

feedbacks from countries like France, Germany, Belgium, and modified its strategy for communication with the client and worked on it, mostly on the customer highlighter weaknesses. The focus was placed on continuous communication with the customers on the aspects of improving-accuracy and ease of understanding issues, response time, and overcoming the blur caused over long-term contracts. The new strategic plan ensured that companies

- use communication to solve existing glitches and problems.

- make courtesy calls to clients to check if there was ambiguity in contracts and clarify them.

- send client notification about extension of request processing.

- find solution to any misunderstanding that the client might have had.

The significance of carrying out this long-term permanent communication strategy was to assure the client that his requests have been addressed or are under process. In-case of an extended deadline, the client was informed in advance. Implementation of this changed communication strategy greatly enhanced customer attitude in Germany, and made them extremely happy. In other countries customers expressed expectation of being served following a similar strategy, where it becomes easier to renew their expired contracts.

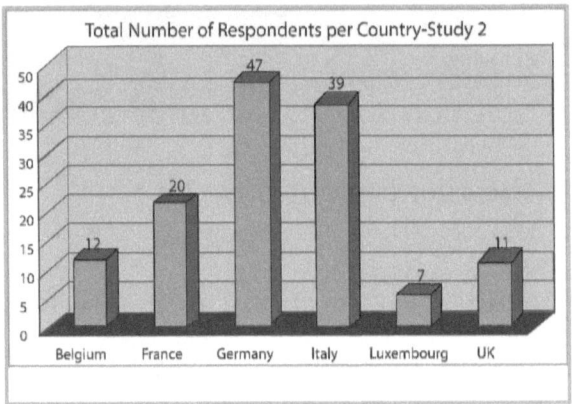

Figure 3

After implementation of this new customer strategy, post-September 2011, in March 2012, the customer's opinion was again sought via online questionnaire in study 2- containing the same questions used in the first online study. Here is the total number of respondents per country as shown in Figure3.

Results of study 2: The same questions

placed forth the customers in study 1 was once again sent to customers who had participated in the first study, besides a few other customers who had not participated before. And 144 respondents answered the questions this time, which was much higher than the first study- 12 clients responded from Belgium, 28 from France, 47 for Germany, 39 from Italy, 7 from Luxembourg and 11 from the UK, respectively, as shown in Figure 3. The overall responses from all countries indicated that 48% of the responses were in the top of the scale, and 21% on the lower scale.

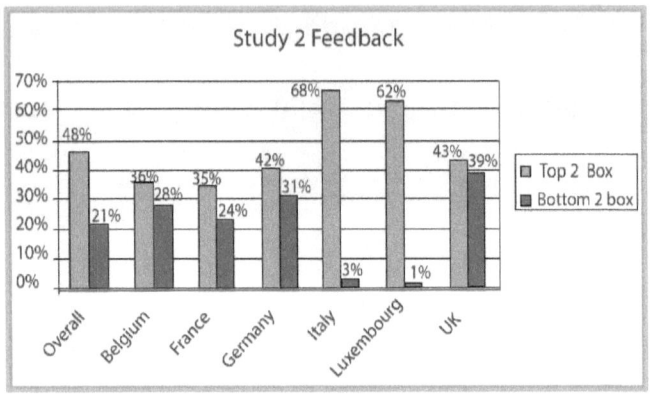

Figure 4

36% of Belgian responses were at the top of the scale, and 28% at the lower scale; 35% of the French responses were at the top and 24% at the bottom; 42% of German responses were found at the top of the scale, and 31% at the bottom. Italy presented 68% positive responses and 3% negative responses; 62% of the responses from Luxembourg were registered at the top of the scale, and 1% in the lower part. And 43% of the responses from

UK were positive and 39% negative as presented by Figure 4.

To conclude, it can be said that the value of positive responses increased overall, even for those countries that had initially given negative responses except Luxembourg, because of disparity between the volume of work and the personnel involved to process customer orders. Evidently, the courtesy calls made by employees helped them reach the target to find out the specific complaints of customers and their remedies as well, initiating appropriate measures to achieve it. However, employees or customer servants of a company should be careful about customers' time, cultural differences etc and ensure clarity and precision in the message during a courtesy call. The employees of the organisation successfully understood the customer's needs and complaints being empathic. They adopted a positive attitude of *'I can handle it'*, to quickly resolve their problems by improving upon their contract administration services, which increased the chances of the customers collaborating further with the company. The communication strategy has been effective and its impact felt upon by the customers though customers of different nations provide different layers and levels of information due to the cultural differences they have.

Antonio Neri, CEO of Hewlett Packard is initiating many cost-cutting measures due to the global pandemic of Covid 19 due to eroding sales. This business technology giant plans to carry out major business renovations, including employee layoffs, which would enable it to save $1 billion by 2022. The company which excels in making data centre hardware and software announced its future plans on Thursday My 21st 2020 while the second quarter fiscal earnings were being announced.

One of the major components of the plan is temporarily slashing employee salaries from July 1st to October 31st 2020, which would affect the executives the most. This would be the real test of time to see whether the company as driven by the ideals of Dave Packard since its inception can function properly with its lofty ideals as before.

Communication Impact

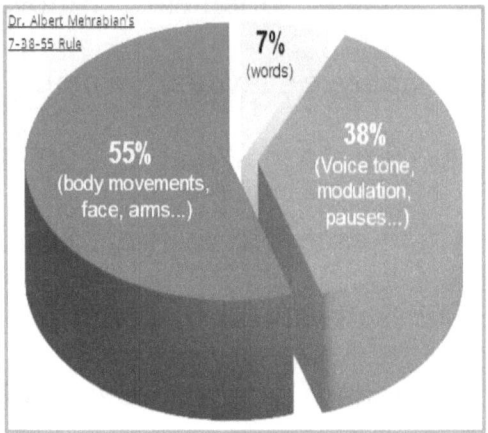

Professor Mehrabian through two studies statistically established that total impact of any communication is centred around-

→ 7% on the words used

→ 38% on the volume, tone & pitch of voice, rate of speech, modulation, etc.

→ 55 % on body language namely facial expressions, gestures and postures, as well as visual language expression.

Each of the above aspects of communication is an essential attribute of creating an excellent customer experience.

Using verbal and nonverbal communication:

Despite how one intends to transfer the meaning of a specific message with definite objectives, every kind of communication can be classified as verbal or nonverbal. And again, both verbal and nonverbal communication can be categorized as vocal and non-vocal, though a major portion of communication that happens between two or more communicators comprises of words in a particular language. Vocal verbal language involves words and, therefore, voice, while nonvocal verbal communication involves communication expressed through written words, sign language, finger spelling, Braille, and other alternatives for verbal language. So while serving customers, it's important to have sufficient awareness and understanding of their background to create a wonderful customer experience through appropriate choice of words in language as necessary. The different components of Nonverbal communication are:

- Tone of voice

- Pitch and volume of voice

- Speech rate

- Articulation of words

- Rhythm, intonation, pause and stress placed on words (modulation)

- Facial expression

- Span of eye contact made

- Gestures, touch, postures

- Body language

It's possible that either you or your customer is suffering from hidden stress during a service interaction or have sensed a suppressed tension prior to it. It would better to defer that interaction in that case.

However, if it is impossible under the existing situation to control that customer experience by delaying the moments of interactions, focus on shrinking your own stress level by being more aware of your thoughts. Avoid distractions by concentrating on the present and controlling your facial expressions by stepping down on the reactive thoughts. An open, focused mind full of curiosity for things being said or to be said by the other person involved in the communication would enable one to have more control over eye movements. Verbal signals should be consistent with verbal expressions; hence paying attention to any inconsistency in communication would ensure providing a better customer experience.

Using different types of verbal communication:

Verbal communication includes both written and oral communication. Oral communication uses both aural and visual means such as - telephone calls, interviews, teaching/training, delivering presentations, negotiation, meeting, audios and videos, group discussion, etc.

Written communication involves the use of pen and paper as well as technological devices such as in- pen & paper letters and documents, emails, SMS, text chats, electronically typed documents of different kinds as well as messages conveyed through electronic devices using sins and symbols. Every piece of communication has a definite objective, and can be broadly categorized under -

1. Interpersonal Communication

2. Intrapersonal Communication

3. Public Communication

4. Mass Communication

5. Small Group Communication

Communicating with the customer can be *interpersonal*, *public*, or in a *small group*. Therefore, it's important for the communicator to be aware of his/her level of **assertiveness**, **passiveness** and **aggressiveness** to create a positive consumer experience.

Passive	Passive-Aggressive	Aggressive	Assertive
√ Respectful	ø Respectful	ø Respectful	√ Respectful
√ Appropriate	ø Appropriate	ø Appropriate	√ Appropriate
ø Honest	ø Honest	√ Honest	√ Honest
ø Direct	ø Direct	√ Direct	√ Direct
Others' needs are the priority.	Neither person's needs are met.	Your own needs are the priority.	Needs are equal.

Using body language as an essential

component of communication

Great customer communication is an acquired

or learned skill and non-verbal

communication plays a dominant role in that.

No matter what your usual body language pattern is, while you are handling customer experience, it is of utmost importance that you recalibrate it to create a positive customer feeling. This is because not only your individual survival and existence but also the company's survival and existence depend on it. To read your customer, means you can connect to all their signals, both verbal and non-verbal. You can discard the redundant bits and connect to the rest to create meaning the exact same way he or she might be striving to tell you. You can then use your own verbal and body language to assure the customer that you understand his or her needs exactly.

People meeting for the first time, bear an unconscious tendency to look forward to similarities in patterns of behavior of themselves.This helps them to create a successful bonding to communicate and channel their thoughts and feelings. Hence mirroring or matching subtly and cautiously the customer's verbal language in terms of choice of words, and mostly his or her body language, namely facial expressions, postures and gestures initiates in gravitating that bond, that paves the path for future communication and interaction with them.

Give your complete attention to your customer during communication, while maintaining steady eye contact with them. Make them feel you are 100% present with them at the moment and are keen on understanding them. Express your attention by- slightly inclining yourself towards them, facing the customer directly, holding your eye contact without staring at them, but giving them due importance, sustaining a relaxed and open posture restraining your arms from being in a crossed position.

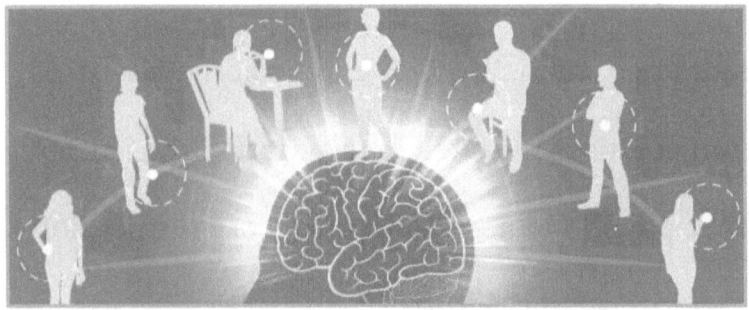

Avoid excessive movement during interactions as it would create negative vibes in your customer about you, as it would reflect mental restlessness pertaining to too many possible thoughts in your mind, that is bound to make the customer feel insignificant and thus would aggravate his/her anxiety at that moment.

Fidgeting during a customer interaction also reflects that the concerned executive is not focused on the task at hand, that customer dealing.

Maintain an open body posture as it generates an atmosphere of warm welcome and confidence communicating subconsciously your trust and honesty with them. Flash your genuine smile and keep a friendly neutral face as it instantly generates warmth and positivity in you, making you easily approachable. Learning to smile genuinely with customers will lead to a significant increase in the number of happy and satisfied customers. Deliberate use of gestures during customer interaction will enhance fluency and articulation, increasing your efficiency and effectiveness in communication. But the gestures must be meaningful and add to effectiveness, not mar it. Keeping an eye on the customer's feet would reveal a lot about the person's emotional state, and thus would contribute more to holding effective communication. A bored, stressed or anxious customer would have his feet oriented towards the exit door showing they are ready to leave, while a customer who is engaged and interested would have their feet firmly directed towards the customer service executive interacting with him/her. A confident handshake at the close of the interaction would make the customer experience memorable to the customer, leaving behind a positive impression. It makes the customer service executive look very professional, competent and confident.

Using your Voice and vocal cords:

The tone of the voice lends the communicator the ability to modify the meanings of words said, by changing the pitch, volume, intonation and the tempo of the voice. This is because, the listener interprets the meaning of the communicator's message using sound, being sensitive to the impact of the tone created during a speech. Though each individual has a unique vocal tone and range of voice gifted to him or her at birth, namely bass, baritone, tenor, alto, mezzo-soprano and soprano, the tone of a voice can be modified to a desirable level through practise to achieve a specific purpose of communication.

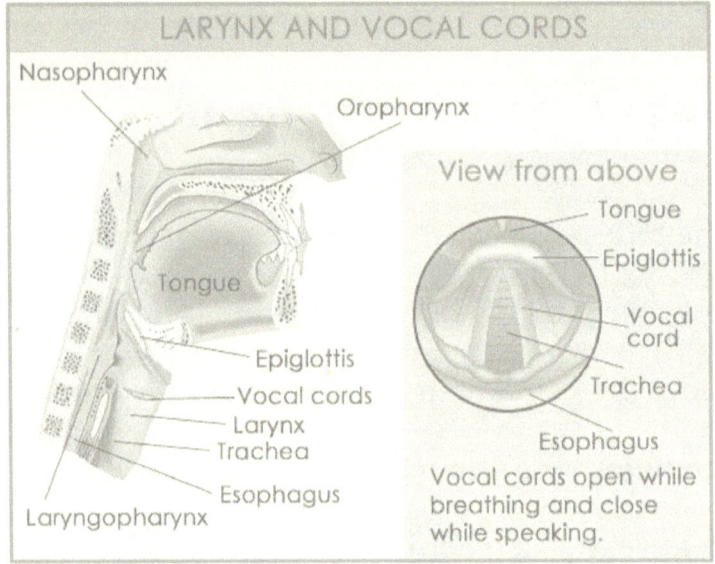

You should hence learn to use your voice and vocal cords carefully to achieve the desired outcome of an interaction.

Mae West, the famous American singer, actress, screenwriter, playwright, and comedian, said, 'It's not what I do, but the way I do, it's not what I say but the way I say'... Known for her light-hearted double entendres, Mary Jane "Mae" West has shown the significance of using the voice and vocal chords that emanate the pitch, tone, volume of the voice judiciously as they greatly impact the meaning of words in a given context of a situation. While interacting with customers, whether in person or over the phone or through writing, the use of proper tone of voice is crucial to the success of communication. Here the choice of words also influences the tone of communication. Despite what you may be saying to your customer, the tone of your voice would reflect your feelings when you say them...and the usage of an incorrect tone of voice might generate negative feelings of irritation, doubt and anger in your listener.

Using a soft, empathetic tone expressing

warmth, humour, passion, or whatever emotions you may like your customer to experience or feel is the essence of a successful communication with your customer. This will particularly soothe and get irate, angry, or upset customers to open up to you and feel heard. Your voice is a very powerful tool of communication as it reflects your emotions and personality. If your customers like your voice and the sound of it, they would form positive impressions in their mind pertaining to your knowledge, confidence and credibility.

2

UNDERSTANDING: THE SCIENCE TO EXCEL IN CUSTOMER SERVICE EXPERIENCE

> *To improve customer experience, move from touch points to journey...Observe, Shape, and Perform.*
>
> -McKinsey & Company
>
> Customer Experience: New Capabilities, New Audiences, New Opportunities (2017)

Every conversation with the customer should aim to analyze and explore into the zone of a customer's needs and expectations. Through all regions and sectors, business organisations and their leaderships realize that a superior customer experience lends a competitive advantage and value to the brand. This advantage and value exist not only in what the customer receives as products or services but also by the method or way through which it is delivered.

In the present-day business scenario, companies not only distinguish themselves from others by product differentiation or efficiency, but also develop unique distinction through creation of a continuous all-round customer experience through the channels of their interactions. And amidst this diversely changing landscape of customer experiences with emerging innovations in technological and other components of the moving market, it becomes inevitable to design customer-centric strategies to create excellent customer experience, leading to customer satisfaction and loyalty.

Knowing what your customers need:

To win over customer satisfaction and loyalty through an excellent customer experience, , it is absolutely necessary to understand your customers and know what they need.

Five Myths about Customer Needs: Sometimes the customers might have difficulty in identifying the exact product suitable for them, or they might not know their exact need during product selection and sometimes they just don't wish to spend time searching for the right products to suit their needs.

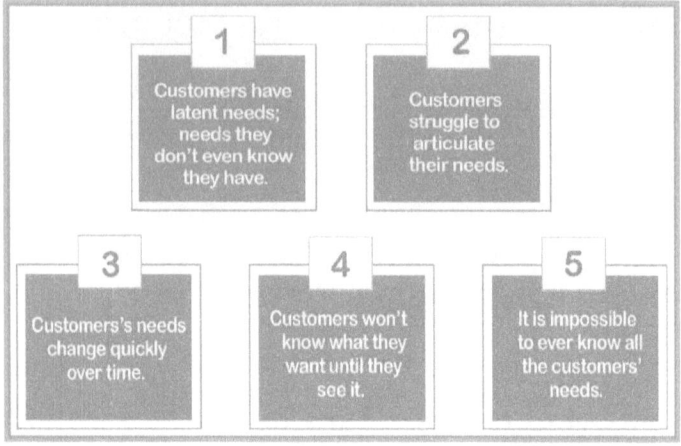

At other times often you may come across a group of customers who, at one point of time would make purchasing decisions or take product related decision on the basis of their instinctive feelings. Again, the same bunch of people on other days may decide to take informed decisions on the basis of facts and data. And some other time, this same group of people might take decisions on the basis of both instinctive feelings as well as facts and data, besides being guided by peer suggestions, advises, or reviews.

Therefore, the business analysts too often stay perplexed as to what might drive a customer's decision-making process as they adopt different measures to decide at different times. Understanding the customer's true needs and expectations in such a situation considering all the changing parameters of time and life is a crucial task. What then could be safe or reliable to generate a great customer experience through understanding his requirement? The clue is *managing your customer expectations by translating his wants into needs and helping him identify his actual needs, thus creating a great customer experience.*

Wants, needs, and expectations as key motivators drive any and every person, and not only the customer. The customer's needs and wants are not identical, and failing to understand them can lure businesses to walk into tempting situations and adopt practices that might jeopardize their interests in the long run. Wants and needs are two aspects of motivation for the customers, which drive them to make their decisions. Hence, understanding and differentiating them is very important.

→ **Need** can be defined as a requirement for that thing that has the capability of solving a genuine or an imagined problem.

→ **Want** can be defined as the urge to possess something, be it for a rational or irrational purpose.

→ **Expectation** can be defined as a projected outcome of a specific decision, namely a purchasing decision.

Expectation is the most significant aspect of understanding the customer, as it involves the journey of the customer from the moment he/she thought to purchase something. Each and every process of interaction that the customer undertakes with the company post thinking about purchasing that item, the expectation grows. Finally when he decides to make that purchase and experiences each and every step of that process, the effect or impact of that purchase digs its roots in him. The customer's wants can frequently be a greater motivator than his actual need. This becomes clearly evident when you request a customer while serving them to specify why they want what they want/seek. In general, the customers have fiery yearning to procure what they want and simply look for ways to get it or would ask you to tell them how to get it. Hence to know the customer's need better, look into their perspectives. However, it is also important to manage customer expectations by solving existing common and potential issues, maintaining transparency while providing information, setting clear timelines, being realistically optimistic, and following up with them.

Looking into their perspectives:

Customer experience leaders can employ advanced analytics to have a clear perception about creating customer loyalty; however, it calls for a lot of patience and courage to train an organization to perceive the world from the customer's perspectives. It takes a lot of effort to redesign organizational functions to create value from a customer-centric perspective. The customer support or customer care or customer service department plays the most significant role here, helping customers unable to identify or face challenges in finding the product or service they want or need because they are unaware. Here the customer service desk of the organisations can listen attentively and actively to the customer's queries and requests, direct them towards their actual needs using appropriate questioning skills, and identify the nodal points of differences to distinguish between the customer's wants and needs. Asking the right questions is the most important thing here as customers themselves cannot differentiate between their wants and needs. The sentences "I need a new laptop" and "I want a new laptop" may apparently mean the same thing semantically.

However, it is the approach with which the customer service desk would analyze these two sentences using appropriate questions that would clearly help both the customer service executive as well as the customer to understand the difference between their want and need, and make purchasing decisions focused on their need. It is only when both the customer and the customer service Executives have been able to differentiate between the want and need of the customer, through the various touch points and the processes, that they can find a solution to address the need of the customer, guiding the customer to make his/her purchasing decision.

Finding a solution for them :

Ewan Duncan says, "In order to rewire a company to become a customer-experience leader—for most companies, this will be a two-to-three-to-four-year journey. The reason it takes so long is, quite frequently you need to work across functions, geographies, and customer segments, and it just takes a while. You need to start where you can show impact quickly before you can scale. Once you succeed, though, you'll have a competitive differentiator that others will find hard to match." Therefore, to find a solution to the customer's need looking into it from their perspectives across diverse functions, geographies, cultures, and customer segments, it's important to understand their psychological biases and remove the barriers held there to arrive at a solution through a proper customer need analysis. Some customers might be unskilled at articulating their needs, some might be non-conversant with terminologies and industry jargons of business products and services, some might have confusing wants and needs while having endless access to a great pool of information online about the product, while some might be hesitant on sharing information with you.

To see what solutions they are looking up to, conduct customer need analysis surveys which the customers can respond to online or respond to verbally they are on physical touch points. Here are a few things to consider while creating surveys.

✓ Keep the language simple and straight, unambiguous and focused on the needs of the customer and not on the company, so they bring out the decisions of the customer easily that get translated into business actions. Customers think in terms of taking decisions to obtain more value for less price and lesser effort, and not in terms of sales cycles, value propositions, USP, marketing funnel, etc.

✓ Collect data through a few questions, as smaller surveys contribute better in identifying challenges within a shorter span of time. Avoid asking irrelevant and misleading questions.

✓ Avoid asking complex questions. Use a few basic or fundamental questions to analyze aspects of customer satisfaction, loyalty and a few other relevant questions for that survey.

Ensure that your questions deal with fixing issues and finding solutions to existing problems.

✓ Focus appropriately on the *whom* and *how,* than *how many* in the survey, as the target segment and the methods of survey are more important than the sample size in particular. It is possible that a small sample size result can be biased, misleading or useless as representation becomes precise and different. Surveying a wrong target group and depending on the outcome can be suicidal.

✓ Ensure there are no confusing and challenging questions, and a few questions to identify whether the person taking the survey belongs to your target group would be beneficial in procuring correct data. Forced-rank questions contribute to identifying what is important to the respondents, although ranking more items, particularly when there's a lack of strong opinion amongst the respondents, becomes challenging for them. The top-task approach produces better results here when you rank more than a few question items in the survey.

✓ Ensure that the survey doesn't become too hard for the person/customer responding to it. Keep a lesser number of open-ended questions to secure detailed information, and where you need to have more open-ended questions in the survey, mark 'necessary' where you must have an answer; while for others mark it as optional.

✓ Ensure that when your questions are aimed at non-mutual exclusivity and require only one choice to pick up by the respondent, there's only one choice available. A typical example of this selecting age and income brackets.

To understand your customer better and improve customer experience, focus on the complete customer journey and not just on the customer touch-points. **Observe** their perspectives at the various points of their interaction with the company. This would help the companies to **shape** their organization better, focused around customer needs, which will help them to **perform** better as leaders by redesigning their customer experiences, which would establish the organisations as world-class business leaders by reshaping their customer interactions.

Case Study: Walmart Inc. Walmart has proudly placed itself amidst the Fortune 500 companies for the last 25 years, a whole quarter of a century, performing in the 'General Merchandisers' category, occupying the first position for the last seven years consecutively. Comprised of 2,200,000 employees, its primary internal customers, who have gained and retained the trust and faith of its external customers by providing exceptional customer service experience, Walmart is a company without competition. Its fight against Amazon stood it on strong ground in 2018, increasing its US online sales by 40% through enabling of thousands of its stores by arranging for grocery pickup, besides smartly taking advantage of a number of its rival's challenges.

Studying its customers segment by segment and understanding their needs carefully, Walmart has created a unique framework for its customers' journey and is continually organizing and reorganizing itself and mobilizing its employees to deliver consistent value to the customers in line with its purpose.

The company has considered the implementation of innovative ideas like creating personal shopping service experience for its consumers and organizing delivery through self-driving delivery vans. It has focused well on improving the most important customer journey first, being a customer experience leader, managing customer experiences keeping the customer psychology in mind and transforming the digital profiles to remove the difficulties faced during interactions. It has kept the necessary culture of continuous innovation on the move, making more fundamental organizational transformations as and when required.

Walmart stands out the winner for the Omnichannel Report 2019, for the most robust and best-executed features amongst the top retail chains.

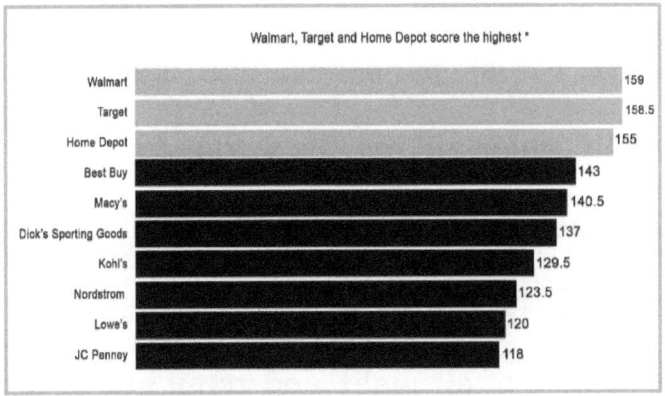

Source-Internet Retailer research 2019

Omnichannel Report

Walmart's success had stretched out to its rising Sam's Club business, and its focus on the few selected key international markets that would propel the company's sales to 3% growth, which would go beyond the $500 billion mark to retain its position amongst the Fortune 500 companies.

However, the gravest challenge that the company has to take in its stride is the recent global health disaster caused by Covid 19 (Corona Virus) pandemic that killed over 250,000 people all over the world, resulting in a crushing global economic disaster due to the global lockdown and social distancing. The closure of all malls and retail stores are bound to impact the purchasing decisions and thought patterns of people, as they are yet to recover from the tremendous mental and financial shock, resulting in a drastic dropdown of the consumerist mindset.

1. Will Walmart be able to survive through these changing times and still hold onto its world-class position as number one in the Fortune 500 list?

2. What suggestions would you give the CEO related to the modification of customer experience, after thoroughly studying the customers' present situation and overall market situation?

3

SERVITUDE: THE ATTITUDE TO WIN CUSTOMER LOYALTY FOREVER

> z*"The key is when a customer walks away, thinking -'Wow, I love doing business with them, and I want to tell others about the experience."*
>
> -Shep Hyken

Servitude - The ultimate goal of every position is serving: While interacting with the customers, the attitude of a business and its people should be one of servitude. This does not mean that the business organization should lose its identity or handover its control to its customers...rather it means, the attitude to serve the customers, the objective of always prioritizing the customer's requirement first by properly analyzing and understanding their needs, and providing them with exactly what they need instead of catering to their wants, and thus win over customer loyalty.

It is very important to walk that extra mile and create that incredible trustworthy relationship that gives customers the wow feeling of carrying out business transactions with a company, and makes them happy enough to pass around and share their consumer experience with others. While interacting with the customers, despite the position a person occupies within the organization, the ultimate goal of the person involved in a specific position within an organization should be serving the customer and providing them that extra something besides the value against their time or money.

Being ready to serve always:

It is the work attitude of the people within the business. Customers notice and remember the behaviour imparted to them and how they felt at that specific moment, which influences their long-term business transaction decisions. We primarily live in the world of feelings, and no matter how advanced technologically the society becomes, businesses rise and fall riding on the waves of the human emotions and their ability to tackle the feelings that arise on particular sensitive moments.

While observing the customer, notice their needs and make out time to determine whether their need calls for an immediate solution or whether it is simply a challenge where they need you to help them address it. It might be supporting them with a little bit of information that they urgently require, or help them resolve a product or service-related issue by addressing their requirement and helping them dissolve their anxiety, or helping them out on an unexpected extra thing that contributes to making their day.

Helping your customers when they are not

even aware that they need your help becomes more meaningful to them than being kind and helpful. If you can keep yourself on high alert and discover what they need drawing from your experiences even before they know it, or if you can empathise with them seeing their challenge from their perspective, they will definitely spread good words around about their experience with you, which would benefit the business and add to its brand value. An employee of a renowned hotel in Paris once noticed that the bright sunlight in the hotel's courtyard often dazzled their visitors who squinted or shaded their eyes from the bright light. Sunglasses of various make were provided there so no more visitors suffered because of the bright sunlight in the courtyard. A small memorable intervention can create a long-term, meaningful relationship.

Delivering superior service:

Customers come with a wide range of expectations- sometimes as promised by a company, sometimes carrying their own bouquet of demands. Set the customer expectation straight, retaining the attitude to serve. However, when and if things go wrong, an apology and remedy to the situation would not repair the damage done. The customer then needs to be made to feel even better than before by delivering additional superior service. A customer that has purchased a faulty electronic gadget is entitled to an apology and a replacement or refund depending on the company's policy. However, it won't mend the dent caused to customer experience, and the customer might break off the relationship chord, leading to a negative word of mouth.

An additional gift voucher or a discount coupon on the next purchase from the store would not only make the customer happy washing out the previous experience, but also would bring him/her back to the store ready to do business once again, receiving service beyond their expectations. Research has shown that customers might transfer their loyalty to a competition, even if they are completely satisfied with a product or service, without an excuse. So creating an opportunity to retain and hold on to their loyalty always proves fruitful.

Creating satisfying customers:

Ensuring that its customers are finally satisfied with their services should be the ultimate goal for every business for winning the long-term game. Hence businesses keep implementing innovative strategies every now and then to keep their businesses operative at the optimal level while staying engaged with their customers. As an employee of the organisation providing a personal touch to all interactions with the consumers is essential in the fast-paced world today. Companies need to ensure that they do not treat their customers just as a number in their sales figure and therefore staying engaged with the customers as individuals in person or in the social media honestly, punctually and realistically. Taking a personal interest in the customers' areas of interest and letting them know that the company cares for them, whether through social networking sites or through the small screen digital modes is a good way of staying connected. It is important to identify, recognise and respond to the customer's journey paying attention to their end-to-end experience journey from their perspective to keep your customers happy and satisfied and win over their loyalty forever. Focusing on all the progression of a customer journey touch-point is more significant than concentrating on individual points of contact and interactions. Knowledge and application of behavioural psychology during customer interactions, with a strong desire and intent to satisfy their need during each interaction by specifically quantifying the need contributes immensely towards creating customer satisfaction. While urging the employees to develop an attitude of 'servitude', companies must remember that their employees are also their primary internal customers, without who the company can never reach out and establish a connection and maintain a relationship or conduct business with the external customers. So the employees must be treated with equal respect and dignity with which the company would treat its external customers. The company must ensure that they are not subjecting their employees to a larger mechanism of oppression, where the employees get victimised by the enormous power of the individual customer where they get the opportunity of making unreasonable demands, and the employee lies defenceless against such claims due to faulty policy or practices.

Case Study: Apple

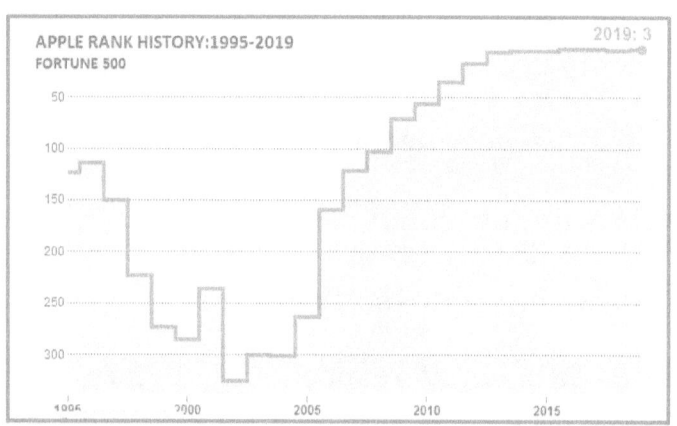

Apple is a luxury product manufacturer and stands as a symbol for social status and class, where its cheapest product range starts at $329 and hi-end products move around $999. Being one of the most successful businesses in the world, the company has been providing exceptional software services and strong technological products besides their accessories. Headquartered in California, Apple launched its first computer in 1976, and since then has grown as a technology giant till date with its iPhones being the most successful amongst its all other products. Apple sold 217 million iPhones in 2018, and occupies the third position amidst the Fortune 500 companies.

Yet it does not enjoy a very happy customer association, who unequivocally speak about the annoyance Apple causes its customers.

They point out that Apple does not sell high-quality products as there is always another product of a similar or higher quality available at a cheaper price, who cater to customer's requirements better than Apple. Here's a few opinions shared about the company's products and service experiences by users: https://www.reddit.com/r/unpopularopinion/comments/apc2zj/apple_is_a_terrible_company/, which doesn't reflect a bright picture about Apple's consumer experience.

Apple is a leader in the world's technological innovations with iPhone, iPad, Mac, Apple Watch, and Apple TV, and software platforms like iOS, iPadOS, macOS, watchOS, and tvOS. It serves that niche customer area having deep pockets and can afford their products to enhance their personal brand, without bothering about the amount spent on Apple products. It also sells products to buyers who can afford Apple products, but seek value for money, and who Apple sadly leaves in a discontented state being number three in the list of Fortune 500's.

Apple has been facing and creating lots of issues for its stakeholders, and the press release it shared in the public digital space on April 30, 2020, indicates that despite enjoying rank three, the company could be facing serious business adversities as the outcome of the Covid 19 pandemic, though it caters to fulfilling the requirements of the rich only. The PR is available here for reading –

https://www.apple.com/newsroom/2020/04/apple-reports-second-quarter-results/. A detailed SWOT analysis of Apple has been carried out by Business Strategy Hub and provided here in this link - https://bstrategyhub.com/swot-analysis-of-apple-apple-swot-2018/; but –

1. Would Apple be able to redesign its customer experience to retain its present rank and climb further up the ladder?

2. Can it address the customers' needs and satisfy them? What strategies could work better in the present world business scenario?

4

TOLERANCE: THE KEY TO BUILDING LONG-TERM CUSTOMER RELATIONSHIP

> *"The responsibility of tolerance lies with those who have the wider vision."*
>
> – George Elliot

Listening is crucial and essential to good communication amongst individuals. In interpersonal relationships, listening turns out to be more successful when carried out actively and empathically. Listening consists of four phases as a complete process. They are-receiving, interpreting, recalling, evaluating, and responding, and involves the following techniques to ensure that the things said have been completely understood. These are –

✓ maintaining eye contact,

✓ not interrupting the speaker,

✓ making encouraging comments/ non-verbal gestures,

✓ formulating appropriate questions,

✓ paraphrasing, and

✓ summarizing.

Practiced without empathy, listening just

becomes an empty and inauthentic set of techniques. No one likes to be taken for granted, whether the employee of a company or its customer. Feeling unappreciated can make one feel bitter, and the communication barrier creeps into a customer interaction, making misunderstanding inevitable there. Misunderstanding leads to the communication gap and can make someone aggressive and irate, especially a customer. No matter how irritating or aggressive a customer turns out to be during a business interaction, it is important to manage that customer by being empathic.

Managing aggressive customers through endurance:

While interacting with a customer who shows aggressiveness, maintain calm and poise and avoid the "fight or flight" response. It is sensible to avoid arguments and show more endurance and kindness as you may not be aware of the actual reason behind the customer's aggressiveness, and his fear. None ever wins an argument with a customer as it always turns out to be a loss in business. It is important to listen to them with proper attention to find a solution to the problem or an issue. Listening attentively is the key to understanding the challenge feeling it from the heart, and prevents leading to an unfriendly or unreceptive situation. If you have been able to find them a solution by carefully listening to them with patient endurance, lead the conversation or interaction to ensure that they leave the spot or their stand easing out on the situation.

Listening with patience to address their grievance:

Listening is the key to solving any issues, even in the gravest of situations. When a person with a problem in listening is placed where he/she has to listen, generally the outcome is, the listener usually plans how to answer to the speaker, resulting in an unfocused incomplete listening. Some others might be preoccupied with thinking about how to create a good impression on the customer.

However, being patient while listening to a customer during an interaction, while the customers state their issue is absolutely essential to focus while striving to find a solution. Acknowledge that the customer has a problem and the challenge is a genuine one. Once you accept there is a challenge, your brain focuses better on the issue, and looks for a possible solution to it. If you cannot find a solution then and there, whether in a written or oral verbal interaction, you can always request to be given some time to find a solution or get the customer connected with a senior person with more experience who can help find the customer a solution to his/her problem.

Exhibit the scale of Empathy:

Giving an aggressive customer a patient and active and focused listening during an interaction with him would create feelings of empathy. Empathic listening is listening with full concern stepping into the shoes of the speaker. This empathic listening can be measured in *The Active-Empathic Listening Scale (AELS)*. This scale contains 11 items (statements), that measure the three-factor scale of *active-empathic listening* through the three dimensions of listening- sensing (n=4), processing (n=3), and responding (n=4). *Sensing* denotes the listener's capability to understand relational or interactive characteristics of speech; *processing* denotes the perceptive and intellectual features of listening and includes –attending to messages, receiving messages, understanding messages, and deducing or interpreting the messages; and *responding* deals with the behavioral outcome of listening, which includes verbal and non-verbal feedback. All versions of the AELS scale uses a 7-point scaling where '1' **denotes *never or almost never true***, and '7' denotes ***always or almost always true***. Each of the 11 statements usually relates to the participants in a particular listening circumstance or applied after a participant has experienced a specific listening situation. The readings on the 7-point scale would reveal the mental stature of the participant and help him recondition himself for reinstating better listening skills.

Resolving conflict:

A relationship that is healthy is bound to come across conflicts, as two entities in communication should be expected to agree on everything, every time. What is important is to understand how to resolve conflict in a healthy way and not avoid it. A mismanaged or unmanaged conflict can immensely harm a relationship. However, if it is managed in a positive manner with mutual respect towards each other, a conflict strengthens the bond between the concerned individuals. The main causes resulting in discord, disagreement and dispute can be analyzed at the roots if one has acquired the conflict management knowledge and skills, and the existing relationship rejuvenates with strength, happiness and growth, be it a personal or professional one. Conflicts can be resolved through negotiation, mediation, arbitration or litigation depending on the duration of the conflicting issue and its level of seriousness.

During customer interactions, care should be taken to ensure that service communication provides sufficient clarity and precision to ensure a positive and healthy consumer experience where a conflicting situation does not arise. However, if a conflict becomes inevitable, it is of utmost significance to ensure that it doesn't get prolonged and gets nipped in the bud without consuming much time at anyone's end. To provide a positive and excellent consumer experience, it is very important to focus on the communications skills of the persons involved in handling consumer experiences, which sets a positive tone even in the stages of conflict resolution. Interpreting the communication of customers accurately avoiding pulling any further service triggers, the customer interaction teams need to have very strong knowledge and understanding of their ground realities. They need to read the customer's body language, process their tones accordingly, and get the meanings behind the spoken and unspoken words. Frequently what the customers express nonverbally and what they say are not the same and a lot stays hidden under unspoken words. This needs to be dug out by delving deeper into the realms of a customer's minds. This is where the effectiveness of communication lies, which can contribute smoothly to sailing and bailing out of a conflicting situation.

Case Study: Amazon

Amazon ranks 5th in the Fortune 500 list in 2019, climbing up from its previous rank of 8th amongst the 500 companies with a revenue of $232,887.0.

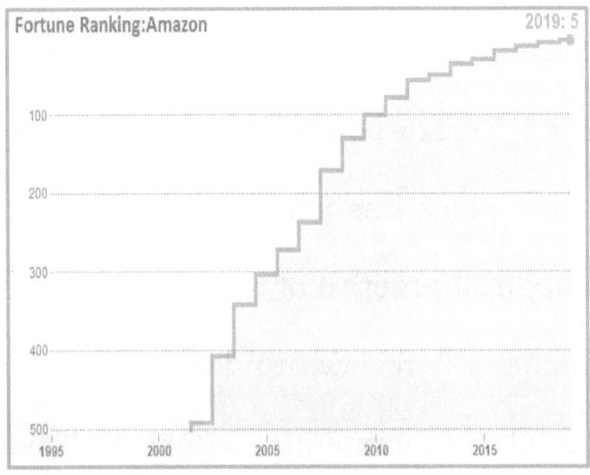

Amazon's growth has been massive in 2018 and the company made huge profits on its leading software business, Amazon Web Services. Jeff Bezoz's Amazon has been operating as an online bookseller since 1994

and it surmounted as an unparalleled e-commerce business without competitor, which either made meagre profit margins or lost all of its money. However, it has become unbeatable in everything 'from bundled memberships of free and speedy retail delivery and original video programming to ground breaking Alexa-powered Echo digital assistants. This has become possible due to the company's practice of listening intently to the customers' review, understanding their needs and requirements better, and being tolerant towards their opinion or suggestions no matter how they get placed. Amazon follows a zero-tolerance policy towards any kind of violations in any customer reviews and leaves no scope for any kind of manipulative attempts in those. It pays great attention to the customer's feedbacks and takes stringent measures on its seller's selling privileges if any manipulative effort gets detected.

However, Amazon's lack of tolerance towards internal customers, its employees and their unhappiness about working in the environment provided is well known. It is a very tense place to work in as far as the corporate culture is concerned. This link would provide more insight:

https://www.beckershospitalreview.com/hospital-management-administration/9-key-issues-with-amazon-s-corporate-culture.html

Had Amazon shown more tolerance towards its employees and sellers treating them as majestically as it does its customers, there would be lesser challenges. Understanding their issues as well and taking up better measures to resolve the conflicts in their day to day collaborative partnership mode of business, , there would have been better boost to its business.

5

OWNERSHIP: THE ESSENCE OF BUILDING A BRAND

> *"Take ownership of every decision you make, because you will be held responsible for the film, whether good or bad."*
>
> – David Fincher

'Ownership' can have diverse meaning and needs to be applied to a specific context. Ownership in the workplace refers to owning up the responsibility towards an organization's product or services as one's own and taking full accountability of its quality. Similarly, taking ownership while handling customer interactions implies taking complete accountability of the company and the customer's interactions as your own and telling them both, in words or in silence, "You can trust me to do all that it takes." Accepting accountability is taking responsibility for the outcome. When your customers buy from you, despite the fact whether they are individual male, female or organisational buyers, you get to know what industry are they from and their financial size to better read their expectations. Understanding the reason behind their buying would help you successfully handle the deal and take better care of any probable issues that might arise later.

Taking full responsibility for any issue:

Depending on the nature of our business and the kinds of customers that you could attract, take complete responsibility of the interactions you have with them whether you interact through a website or a one-on-one meeting, to make them feel good. See what gets them to open up so you can serve them the way they want. Focusing on their budget sell them what they can afford, clearly mentioning any possible shortcomings, understanding on the process if they will open their purse a little wider. However, if they are unwilling to extend their budget, assure them you will be there to help them out if any issues occur later.

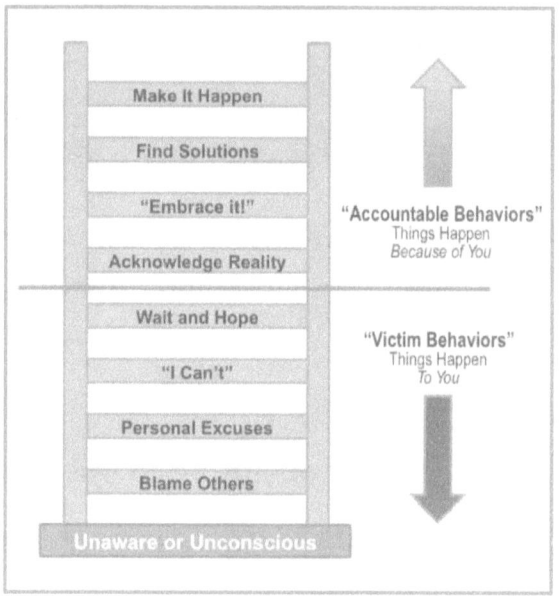

Understand whether the customers expect a dependable delivery, or they are looking up to post purchasing services, and in that context how do they view your competitor. If you successfully cater to all their expectations without violating or adding discomfort to the existing policies of your company, your customers are more likely to buy more from you in the future. If an issue crops up with the product or service, acknowledge it, being empathic with the customer and tell them clearly what you can do about it to address the issue. If the redressal requirement doesn't get covered in the warranty period, tell them so politely and mention you could talk to someone to find out how the issue can be solved in a cost-effective way. A Marriot Courtyard at Mississauga had a customer showing up who had accidentally booked his room in the following month. There was no room available at the hotel to accommodate the visitor, but the employee of the hotel didn't show him a cold shoulder or shrug him off. But rather, she owned up his problem as her own and called up the hotels nearby to search and find him a place to put up at that moment. Ownership has a much broader meaning attached to it. It definitely is your choice to decide how much you want to own it up and apply it to your context, looking up at the bigger, brighter picture.

Avoiding the blame game:

If you are not sure how to solve an issue, simply avoid pointing your fingers at someone else. Find out if someone else has the solution to an issue that can save the customer trouble. The typical mindset that usually comes up when something goes wrong is blaming others and not owning up the responsibility on oneself.

Stephen Covey said, '*Accountability breeds response-ability.*' Accountability applies to everyone in each and every rank within an organization, and is used to signify personal responsibility for getting a preferred outcome. The image of the accountability ladder above shows that the higher on the ladder one is, the more reliability and responsibility one would have, resulting in better performance and productivity. And, the lowest in the rungs of the ladder one is, the least *consciousness* or *awareness* they have, without even understanding that a particular circumstance needs to be dealt with. At the level of *blame*, people have some consciousness, but as they bear a victim mindset, they always blame others or find a scapegoat, behaving in the most immature manner. People at the levels of giving personal excuses and expressing their inability to do something reflect the behavior of adults who refuse to grow up 'psychologically'. Solely based on their own imaginations, they build up their belief systems in such a way, that they cannot ever achieve a set task at hand. They do not believe or acknowledge their fault or drawbacks in not achieving the goals but rest their firm belief on external circumstances controlling them. Even people standing their grounds at the 'Wait and Hope' level are captive of the victim mindset, which places the obligations of an outcome on someone or something else.

A strong customer support team that owns up responsibility and avoids blame game can always enhance its customer's trust successfully. Customers having such trustworthy experiences believe that all challenges will be fixed on time and hence express a more receptive behavior if and when trouble springs up.

Case Study: Berkshire Hathaway Inc

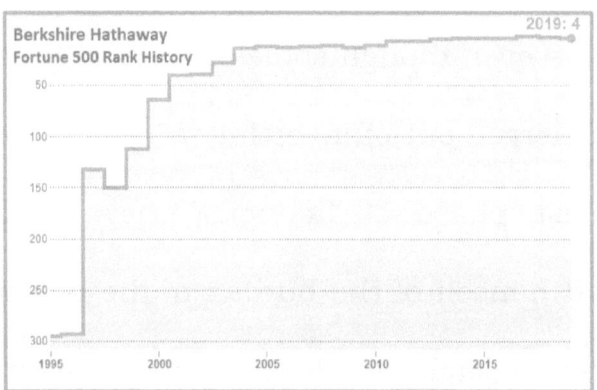

Berkshire Hathaway, led by Warren Buffet, ranks 4th amidst the Fortune 500 companies with a team of 389,000 employees.

With a steady record of being in the Fortune 500 list for the past 35 years, Berkshire operates in the financial sector, handling Industry Insurance of Property and Casualty (Stock). Despite booking a $3 billion loss invested on Kraft Heinz, and falling behind in sales of Apple also Berkshire's largest stock holding, Warren Buffet has not invested in the Covid 19 even though some of his best profits have emerged out of investments made in the gloomiest phase of financial crisis. Buffet relieved himself of the burden of the massive investment loads made in airline companies like American, United, Southwest, and Delta Airlines, which caused massive net loss to Berkshire in the first quarter, as he considers usual flight schedules during the uncertain pandemic phase could change over a long period. Instead, Berkshire Hathaway focused on restructuring its business to provide additional cover-up to support the small businesses badly hit by this uncertain pandemic caused by Covid 19, spread around in Dining, Hospitality & Entertainment; Personal Services & Care; Professional Financial Services; Property Maintenance & Janitorial; Technology & Creative Services; Trades, Repair & Construction; Transportation & Trucking; Retail, Wholesale & More industries. This attitude of responsibility of saving other businesses and creating an opportunity for them to revive and rebuild themselves once again during these dark and challenging moments of the disturbed global economy not only reflects Berkshire Hathaway's attitude to look beyond personal greed and profitability that would safeguard only the organisation's own customers, but also gives the opportunity to other businesses to safeguard the interests of their own employees and their customers as well while assuring customers across different business sectors to be served according to their needs to the best ability possible under the situation.

6

MANAGEMENT: THE CORE COMPONENT OF SUCCESSFUL CUSTOMER SERVICE EXPERIENCE

"Management is, above all, a practice where art, science, and craft meet."

- Henry Mintzberg

Since 2016, over 80% of companies have focused on prioritizing their customer experience, where management of its different components becomes extremely important for providing excellent and effective customer friendly solutions. How companies manage human emotions, whether within the organization or with the people they are carrying out the business transaction, is very important for driving the specific objectives of customer experience.

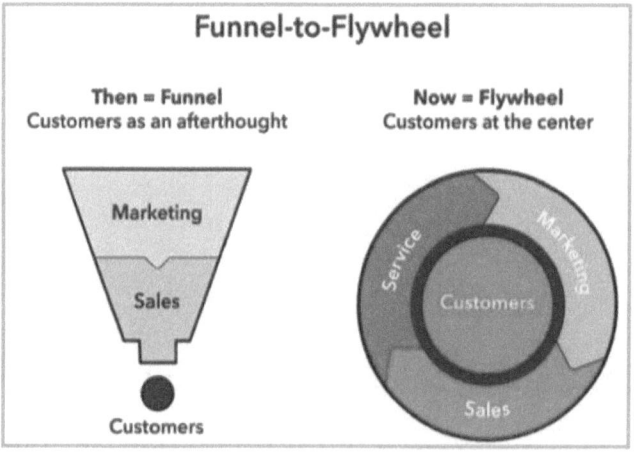

The virtual and physical space of customer interactions also should be adequately taken care of to achieve the desired outcome, besides the management of time from the perspective of the customer and the company.

Managing emotions to deliver long-term successful customer service:

Customers depend on the company for serious as well as simple non-critical solutions and business interactions, which calls for a broad range of 'business continuity management'. Such management skills include managing events that are sudden and unprecedented, to keep systems running end to end managing its security as well, managing risks and alleviating threats.

On such situations, customers do not want to be burdened with reliability issues about technical solutions but invest attention only on their business transactions. They expect the business procedures to be easy to journey through, and they expect to be given an uncompromised listening. It is easy to lose one's emotional control at such tense, intricate and delicate moments, leading to a string of possible disarray and dissatisfaction at all levels – whether internal or external, as people often take things said personally.

If your customer or any internal member of your team mistreats you, do not take their behaviour to your heart and start being judgmental either about yourself or them. You needn't blame yourself for anything or lose your emotional control if people do not give you the respect you deserve and take their behaviour personally. It will cause emotional drainage resulting in a constant re-evaluation of self-esteem. Being reflective and taking things personally continuously are different. Self-reflection leads to self-improvement making one productive while taking things personally leads to the destruction of self-belief and esteem. When you stop taking things personally, you gain more self-control over your responses, your emotions and your overall energy level.

Managing the virtual and physical space

of customer communication:

Your customers expect you to be available to them at their terms and on their time... whether through emails, chats, voice mails, voice calls, messages or other virtual portals. They also expect you to be available on the points of physical contact at customer support centers or their first point of interaction with you whether over the phone, on a store or any other virtual space. They expect their queries or issues to be responded to immediately in a timely manner without wasting time or having to repeat their questions or having to wait for a long time to receive an answer. Therefore, it's important that you make available most probable questions priorly made available on the portals to the customers who want to be served over multiple digital and personal ways through open communication channels. Ensure that you manage your virtual space of communication as well as physical space of communication efficiently balancing between time efficiency and information efficiency.

You also need to decide while rolling out specific information as to 'how much' you are going to say so that the customer comes back to you with repeat business and stays loyal to you. Personal communication between two human beings one-on-one helps the company to retain long-term sustainability because all business in this world happens because of emotional connection...which must not be lost at any cost.

Therefore, how you manage the entire business atmosphere while transacting or interacting with the customer is very important. Keep options for customizing such communication on case to case basis. Use collaborative service partnering where you cannot solve the clients' problems directly and/or hold audio-visual web conferencing where necessary if a challenge needs resolution through interaction and support from two or more persons. Simply ensure that your customer leaves with a happy experience at the end of the interaction leaving scopes for you to reach out again and there can be reconnection whenever required without any hard feelings at any end.

Managing your time and communication

to achieve a desirable objective:

"Time is money"...as the adage goes, making all keep a tag on how you manage your time. Time is the most essential and valuable thing on earth and when time gets lost, we do not get it back to renew an experience by rewinding our tape of life. While serving customers, you might come across people who go about in circumlocutive conversations or going around the same thing again and again. You should understand whether the customer's challenge is actually serious or whether he/she/they cannot communicate what they are looking for. In such situations, cut short the conversation with either crisp to the point questions or show them to the table of someone better equipped to handle such cases and customer needs, ensuring that you manage everyone's time judiciously. Irate and aggressive customers often waste a lot of valuable organizational time, which hinders business productivity. To cool their agitation, first thank them for drawing your attention and listen to them intently, repeating only the issue after them retaining your own calm. Then let them know what you will do to resolve the issue sincerely, giving the highest priority to the case and setting up a specific follow-up time. Ensure that you do not spend too much time hovering over the problem and clear off your mind after you have dealt with the customer so the problem does not linger in your head for a minute longer than necessary, saving your own time and that of the company's within its premises. Also, ensure that you do not carry your official/professional mental baggage home, allowing it to eat up your family time.

Case Study: Amazon Prime Day Why is it the world leader in Customer Experience

Chelsea Hunersen mentions in the blog qualtrics.com that Amazon Prime Day is the world leader in customer experience, and the reason that is evident behind is, efficiently managing the experiences of its customers.

Amazon has been serving its customers for over two decades now with an almost unparalleled product portfolio at competitive prices, making it a legendary business brand combining customer experience and product, which makes the customers coming back every time. To be at this legendary position as **the world's biggest online retailer**, Amazon has had to deftly manage

a. Delivery and Returns

b. Digital Service Experience

c. Product Experience

d. Its service-oriented *Experience* brand 'Zappos', which claims to deliver 'happiness' believing in its mantra, "Powered By Service"

To manage all of the above important components of customer experience, Amazon has efficiently managed its customer's emotions, time, virtual and physical face of communication and interactions. It has reorganized its delivery options through online retail order as well as enabling physical order and delivery through its brick and mortar stores.

A detailed study of – *Amazon Bookstores, Amazon Go, Amazon Fresh,* and *Amazon Restaurant* would clearly provide a better highlight of the company's business operations. Amazon has implemented a lot of technological innovations to improve upon the User experience in the ordering and Return options, as well as the digital experience of the customers online too. Amazon's active customer interactions through its App and the social media faces have greatly affected customer experience, and its product experience coupled with the unique and excellent customer experience have left Amazon happily sitting on the Fortune 500 list surrounded with a happy customer base.

7

EXPERIENCE: THE KEY TO CONVERT MEDIOCRE SERVICE TO OUTSTANDING CUSTOMER EXPERIENCE

> *"The customer experience is the next competitive battleground."*
>
> - Jerry Gregoire

The most significant break that any business in competition can get is through its customer service, which can contribute to creating a large, loyal base of returning customers that lend it long-term survival. And this can only happen if the business can create a unique and excellent customer experience. Though many consider customer service and customer experience to be the same thing, it is not so in reality.

Customer Experience briefly expressed as *CX* has been distinctly demarcated previously as the experiential interactions that customers have with a business throughout their journey during a business transaction, from the ensuing of the first contact with the business till the customer turns out to be a happy and loyal customer as an outcome. However, if the customer match has not been perfect, it is better not to waste much time on that customer and stay more focused on target marketing on potential customers that are the perfect fit for your product or services.

Building positive experience that reflects the company's personality:

The reason so much importance is attached to CX is it is an important component of Customer Relationship Management, and contributes to creating a loyal customer base, which brings in repeat business necessary for the long-term sustenance of a business. Without the customer, there can be no business. Studies reflect that, in 2020 and beyond, the number one brand differentiator will be customer experience. One out of three customers will leave their loved brand if they have one negative experience. Customers have shown a willingness to bear a 13% to18%

premium price towards luxury items and indulgence services if the customer experience is great. And 49% of customers have done impulsive buying just because they received a better personalised customer experience. Companies that receive a high customer experience score (10/10) are likely to spend 140% more and stay loyal for nearly six years.

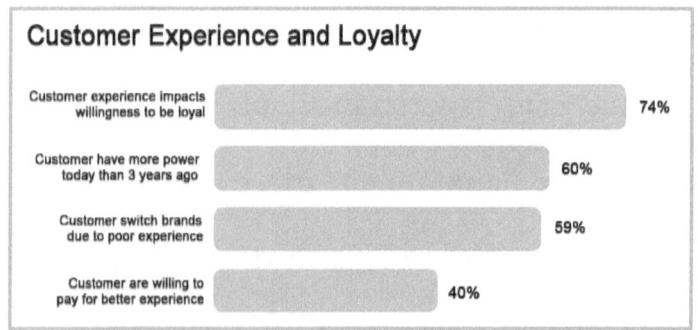

A positive experience would always bring the customer back for more, and Oracle's global study brings out the notions that three-quarters of senior executives rely on positive customer experience greatly impacting the enthusiasm of a customer to be a loyal promoter of any business. This is why businesses need to invest in the experience of their customers to have them stay loyal to the businesses by building positive experiences throughout the customer journeys.

Creating pathways to get a returning customer:

As businesses cannot exist without customers, companies rely heavily upon winning over new customers and retaining them long-term, devising unique CX strategies, creating pathways to get returning customers. The basic point of difference between companies that grow and those that do not see growth is their ability to retain a customer. It is a proven fact that the stronger a business is on customer retention, the better it is on reaching its business goals.

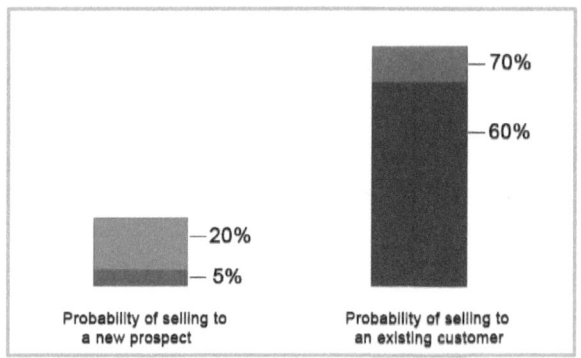

The graph here shows that the money that a business must spend on customer acquisition is much more than it has to spend in retaining that customer. The probability of selling to an existing customer is 60-70% higher and the selling cost to an existent customer is 6-7 times less expensive. However, still companies seem focused more on customer acquisition than customer retention.

But it would be a good idea to focus on customer retention strategies and creating new pathways to retain the old customers, where the first thing to pay attention is – why the customer is leaving. This graph represents a clear picture of why customers leave a company.

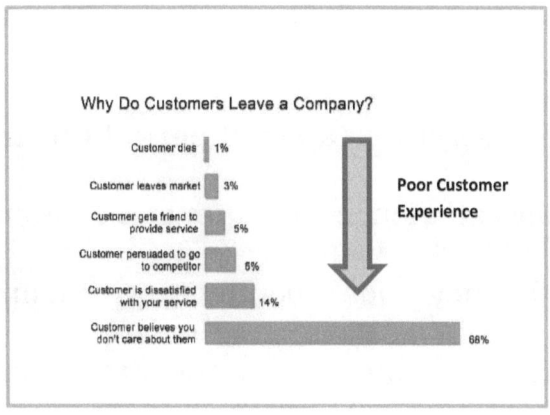

Once you have identified the reason behind the customer leaving, or have noticed churning signs in advance, connect with the customer offering lucrative offers and carry out necessary follow-ups.

Ensure that the follow-ups are personalized and you fulfill whatever promises you have made while making new offers and follow-ups.

Shifting focus from customer service to consumer experience:

Customer service is a small part of the entire customer experience- the sum of a customer's total journey for conducting business. Usually, the customer on the first point of interaction meets an employee of a company, who represents the 'business', and it is where the business gets the first opportunity to provide the potential customer or an existing customer excellent customer experience. Interacting with the customer in a friendly, supportive way is good customer service. However, going a bit extra and creating unprecedented or unexpected positive experience is good customer experience. In the present market system, customer experience has greatly changed and the involvement of technology in business has given businesses the opportunity to connect with their customers in more direct, newer and exciting ways, which has gone beyond one-on-one personal services.

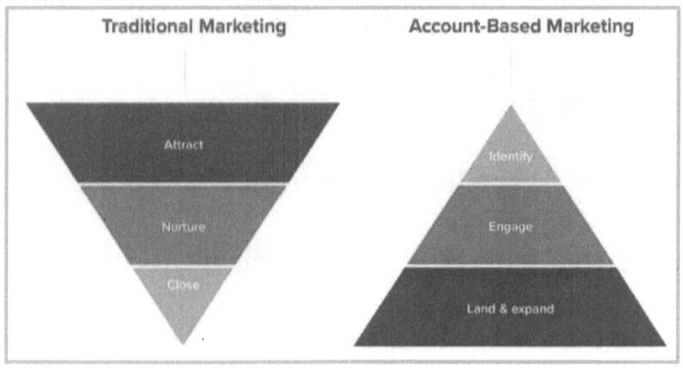

Businesses can better manage customer relationships now, enhancing their experiences using CRM software, which guides them towards future sale predictions depending on customers' previous buying history even before the customer is aware of it. This enables the businesses to predict future needs and requirements of customers, taking proactive initiatives full of attention towards the needs.

The consumer can be made to feel the surging

need for a product or a service through target email marketing, besides understanding their complete viewpoint through CRM driven surveys and other questionnaires that enhance their experiences and enable them to open up to the businesses mentioning their needs and capacities. Customer service, though, still occupies an important role in the customer experience, but the focus has shifted greatly to creating great customer experiences through new technological breakthroughs, which strengthens customer relationships in newer ways, contributing too greater customer retention, which frequently leads to account marketing instead of traditional marketing.

Through this highly focused target sales and marketing, businesses send tailor-made campaigns to customers, where one message is sent to one specific prospective customer.

The difference between an outstanding customer service experience and a mediocre one:

There are quite a few bold as well subtle differences between an outstanding customer service experience and a good or mediocre one. The basic conceptual difference is that, to provide outstanding customer service experience businesses take that extra pain and walk that extra mile to enhance customer experience focused on retaining long-term customer loyalty matched with their business goals. While providing a mediocre or good customer service, the business team is focused on serving the customer only, without caring to focus on the feelings or experiences of the customers to align with their future business prospects and business goals.

Outstanding customer service providers not only strive to keep the customers happy and win over their long-term loyalty, but they also focus on understanding the customers' expectations and serving beyond that, staying within their business policies- or sometimes changing their systems if the customers' need and demands be so. Businesses that provide outstanding customer service experiences treat their customers very specially, valuing their emotions, understanding their needs and wants, valuing their time, providing them that extra service or guidance when they do not realize themselves that they need it. Outstanding customer service providers are excellent communicators and communicate well with their customers, taking proper ownership and accountability of the business, the service experience, and of conflicting situations. A happy and satisfied customer is always bound to make an outstanding customer service experience provider happy and proud, resolving further to serve better, and not become complacent. The area of customer experience needs to be nurtured and taken care of continually with more emphasis on customer experience strategy; only then its impact on customer loyalty, higher customer retention, and increased growth of revenue will be   companies will be appreciated by the companies.

Case Study: Apple's Customer Experience

This image shows Apple's efforts to provide its customers a royal treatment through various measures adopted. Here is the link to the complete infographic:

https://hospitalitymanagementdegrees.net/features/how-apple-stores-give-their-customers-five-diamond-treatment-infographic/

Apple has retained its customer loyalty by 90% in 2018 and could achieve this height by putting intensive effort by working on its customer experience department, before it decided to open its first store. Apple has consistently maintained this effort each time it opened a new retail outlet. Despite possessing enormous resources, Apple did not have to spend a lot of money on delivering excellent customer experience. Small businesses have more advantage compared to larger ones in providing personalized experience. However, Apple superseded that in expectations. Since Apple produces luxury items, superior customer service has increased its revenue turnover compared to Best Buy, Verizon and At & AT.

In 2018, Apple earned a revenue of $35,899,000 per store out of its total 270 stores, while Best Buy made just $34,223,000 per location out of its 1,332 stores, Verizon made $17,515, 000 per location out of its 6,839 stores and At & AT made $13,435,000 from its retail locations having 2,004 stores.

The challenge for Apple is maintaining its rank, although it has a lesser number of real retail stores in different locations compared to its competitors, and continuing to provide excellent experience in the present situation of global economic crisis.

8

RESTORATION: THE NECESSARY QUALITY TO WIN OVER COMPETITION

> *"True Restoration takes patience, subtlety, skill and grace."*
>
> – Paul David Tripp

Restoration in the business context means bringing an existing business state back to its previous state of positive performance, be it on the operational level or any other level.

Business situations are bound to go haywire due to a sudden loss or failure of a critical business function or for the failure of its supportive resources, whether for a natural or man-made disaster, an accident, a sudden emergency or a threat. Whatever be the reason behind the disturbance in business, it impacts both the financial as well as the non-financial aspects, i.e., customer service, creditor confidence, supplier confidence, and overall market confidence. It leads to challenging customer situations within the company sometimes on a daily basis.

Customers in such situations may be distressed or disappointed with product issues, billing problems, or other implementation issues that impact the customers, and the more complex and larger the organisations are, the greater would be the challenges. In such a situation, how can you restore the customers' confidence in the product, service and the organization itself?

Restoring customer's confidence in the product:

Developing a specific approach that can be implemented by all managers designated to ensure customer success and growth in restoration of customer confidence in product/products that have given causes of disputes and dissatisfaction. The basic objective here is taking care of the complicated situations in a manner that makes sure that the customer leaves with a positive impression of the company. Sometimes, such happy customers readily serve as passionate advocates for the same brands in days to come. And to receive this genuine free brand advocacy, all that businesses need to do is be empathetic towards the customers when and if things do not go as expected and products do not work as promised. With empathetic communication, the customer trusts you that the company will work towards resolution. Apologising to the customer after a negative experience they have had also translates that to a positive experience contributing to reviving the confidence of the customer and contributes to satisfactory restoration of the wounded customer relationship. Studies have shown that a genuine apology if it comes from a Customer Success Manager whether on behalf of his department or another department or for the company, expresses a polite, courteous and empathic effort towards the customer which reflects his earnestness to resolve the challenge and strengthens the emotional bond of a customer with the company than a customer who has never experienced any issues with the company. This negative experience turned positive in the customer's journey always contributes to long-term customer retention and regain of the company's goodwill, increasing customer satisfaction by 10-15%.

Restoring customer's confidence in the

organization:

As revealed by a study, an unhappy customer on an average will share his/her negative experience gained from a company with 9-15 people while a heartfelt positive experience would gain the company leverage to win over future markets with ease. In today's technology-enabled world, customers communicate much faster, their thoughts and opinions shared with companies as well as with other prospective customers in the blink of an eye which can be killing as well as rejuvenating for a company. Therefore, every business has an IT team that keeps hunting for customer suggestions and feedbacks online to report to its management team to immediately address an issue or devise strategies to leverage upon positive feedbacks to gain further advantage over its market share.

However, if you come across a negative customer feedback, immediately connect with the customer and offer him a personal apology from your heart amidst a challenging situation, while retaining a positive attitude all the while will restore customer confidence. It will help you salvage your goodwill enabling the business to realise the gains of a strong customer relationship.

Restoring customer's confidence in the

service:

Customer interaction calls for friendly, courteous, helpful, flexible and polite behavior from the person involved in dealing with the customer. Such behavioral attributes are not only nice, positive ones but are desirable qualities especially from leaders dealing with customer success and restoration. During a problem-solving situation, politeness from an employee comes handy in diffusing the issue lying in the customer's mind. When customers feel that the employees of the business have addressed them respectfully with dignity and sensitivity, their feelings of justice and fairness towards the company gets restored and they feel happy about it. A positive attitude is a remarkable asset that greatly affects the confidence of the customer and his/her satisfaction. A resolved customer issue with a rude or indifferent behavior still can cast an ill impact on customer relationship, therefore creating a negative experience. So the simple solution that lies at hand for the customer service team is to maintain a courteous and positive attitude no matter what the situation be so as to deliver a positive customer experience that brings back to the company much stronger loyalty. Treating an existing issue with urgency always helps. A speedy response and resolution of an issue always succeeds in retaining 95% customer loyalty.

The team taking care of customer experience and success must gain the trust of the higher executive members and be enabled with proper training to resolve issues internally across other departments on the first call from the customer or the first contact made. However, if the Customer service management team cannot immediately solve the customer, they should contact the customer immediately to inform them about the possible remedy they are undertaking and the expected turnaround time it would take. It is also important to ensure that any and every business increases its capacity to solve problems quickly, to restore its customer confidence, satisfaction, and loyalty.

Case Study: Amazon Prime

Amazon, the retail powerhouse is a consistent top rank holder simply for its high customer satisfaction. Amazon does not just do lip service but lives up to the promises it speaks about on its website and elsewhere. Amazon's expert knowledge and mode of engagement with customers make it worthy of being mentioned as business delivering excellent customer service and experience.

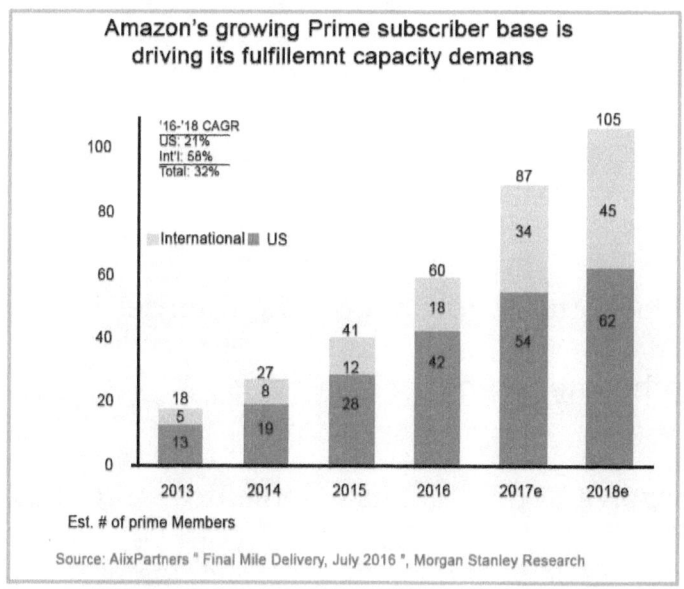

Amazon is fascinatingly quick and trouble-free

in cases of problem resolution. Its efficient service team gathers data from the customer experience by asking them questions and taking their feedback seriously. This helps them improve their customer experience and regain their customer confidence and hold on to customer loyalty. Unhappy customers do not shy away from expressing their doubts on the internet and a single negative customer experience can drive away the new potential buyers, as online buyers always are always on the lookout for reviews on the internet before purchasing a product or service.

Amazon's source *Statista* indicates, '*By 2022 there will be 56 million (i.e., 49%) Amazon Prime Video subscribers alone in the U.S and 122 million worldwide*'.

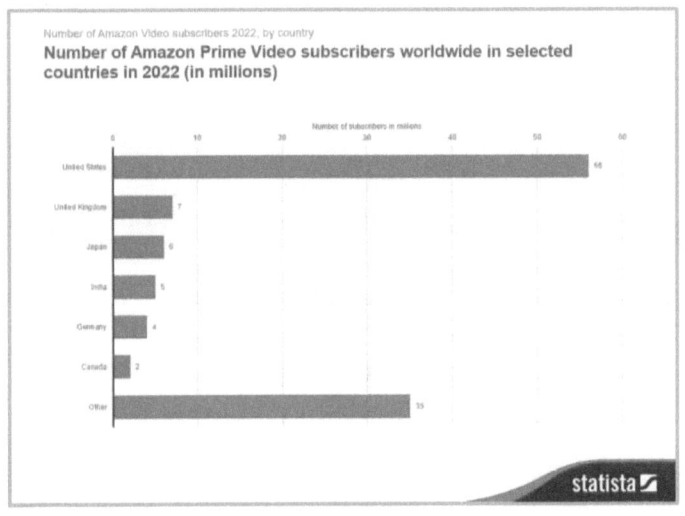

Number of Amazon Video subscribers 2022, by country
Number of Amazon Prime Video subscribers worldwide in selected countries in 2022 (in millions)

'Amazon Prime Video is the primary growth catalyst for Amazon to gain new subscribers in Japan, Germany, and the UK. Amazon Prime membership jumped 16% in Japan in just three months following the launch of Prime Instant Video. Prime subscriber rates increased in the UK and Germany with the introduction of Prime Instant Video.' Source: Amazon Disruption Symposium Where so Far? Where to Next? Who is Safe?, Morgan

Stanley, September 18, 2017.

Restoration of the customer's confidence in the company's products or services is an extension of Jeff Bezoz's Amazon and its business mission and values.

CONCLUSION

> *"People do not care how much you know until they know how much you care."*
>
> —Teddy Roosevelt

In the customer-centric world today, companies must keep customer service as their first priority and not an afterthought. The customer today holds the power to choose who they want to do business with and who they do not want to engage with. This is more than enough to make or break a business in the modern world. Hence business must focus on doing everything they can to acquire new customers, to delight them, and to retain their loyalty. This is why customer experience matters more than customer service.

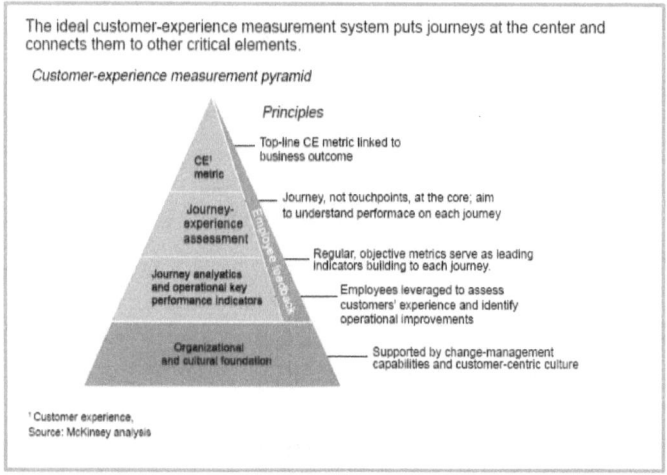

The ideal customer-experience measurement system puts journeys at the center and connects them to other critical elements.

Customer-experience measurement pyramid

Principles

CE' metric — Top-line CE metric linked to business outcome

Journey-experience assessment — Journey, not touchpoints, at the core; aim to understand performace on each journey

Journey analytics and operational key performance indicators — Regular, objective metrics serve as leading indicators building to each journey.

— Employees leveraged to assess customers' experience and identify operational improvements

Organizational and cultural foundation — Supported by change-management capabilities and customer-centric culture

' Customer experience,
Source: McKinsey analysis

Positive customer experience helps a business to retain sustainable growth by enhancing the customer retention rate, for which a businesses must commit themselves to on-going support. Poor customer experience will negatively affect the brand value of a business and negatively affect its revenue, while good service and positive experience would lead to customer loyalty and earn referrals for the business, boosting customer loyalty for a brand. 7 out of 10 US Customers are influenced by businesses that provide them with great services and spend money on them.

Customers want to feel respected and important and expect their feedbacks to be taken seriously, whether provided through surveys or through any other modes. They expect to be kept in the communication loop when something goes wrong, or if the company has made any changes in mode of operations, as they are used to the specific business experiences they have had before and do not want to experience unexpected surprises. So whether a company has added a new service or modified a previous mode of operation, or has committed a mistake, it is important to set the customer's expectation straight by communicating clearly to them and upholding trust and transparency.

Happy Customers............Happy Business!!

Resources

1. https://advisor.morganstanley.com/the-oberheide-group
2. https://www.business2community.com/customer-experience/fortune-500-companies-customer-service-strategy-01685291
3. http://customerthink.com/how-to-take-ownership-in-customer-service/
4. https://www.inc.com/john-boitnott/3-ceos-who-are-using-emotional-intelligence-to-expand-their-business.html
5. https://www.forbes.com/sites/blakemorgan/2019/09/24/50-stats-that-prove-the-value-of-customer-experience/#39044b14ef22
6. https://www.forbes.com/sites/blakemorgan/2019/09/24/50-stats-that-prove-the-value-of-customer-experience/#39044b14ef22
7. https://www.bluleadz.com/blog/companies-with-the-best-customer-service
8. https://fortune.com/fortune500/
9. https://www.forbes.com/sites/blakemorgan/2018/02/15/the-10-most-customer-obsessed-companies-in-2018/#5d91294a6ba1
10. https://www.sciencedirect.com/science/article/abs/pii/S0278431911001587?via%3Dihub
11. https://fortune.com/2020/05/21/hewlett-packard-enterprise-to-implement-major-cost-cuts-because-of-covid-19/
12. https://www.forbes.com/sites/francesbridges/2018/06/29/how-to-stop-taking-things-personally/#313b40ee6726
13. http://www.picturequotes.com/restoration-quotes
14. https://sellercentral.amazon.com/forums/t/new-amazons-customer-product-reviews-policies/421672
15. https://www.sellerlabs.com/blog/amazon-reminder-to-follow-customer-product-review-policies/

16. http://customerthink.com/how-to-take-ownership-in-customer-service/
17. https://fionaparr-focusing.co.uk/patience-and-listening/
18. https://richardbjoelsondsw.com/articles/listening-patience-part-1/
19. https://courses.lumenlearning.com/atd-hostos-interpersonalrelations-1/chapter/listening-chapters-chapter-5/
20. https://richardbjoelsondsw.com/articles/listening-patience-part-1/
21. https://www.researchgate.net/publication/319443851_Active_-_Empathic_Listening_Scale_AELS/link/5a09dc420f7e9bb949f9656d/download
22. https://www.forbes.com/sites/francesbridges/2018/06/29/how-to-stop-taking-things-personally/#3f11f5836726
23. https://www.mdpi.com/2076-0760/6/4/113/htm
24. https://richardbjoelsondsw.com/articles/listening-patience-part-1/
25. https://www.digitalcommerce360.com/2019/02/19/walmart-target-and-home-depot-win-at-omnichannel-retailing/
26. https://www.ukessays.com/essays/business/the-issues-of-apples-article-business-essay.php
27. https://www.reddit.com/r/unpopularopinion/comments/apc2zj/apple_is_a_terrible_company/
28. https://www.apple.com/newsroom/2020/04/apple-reports-second-quarter-results/
29. https://bstrategyhub.com/swot-analysis-of-apple-apple-swot-2018/
30. https://www.berkshirehathaway.com/govern/govern.html
31. https://fortune.com/2020/05/04/some-are-investing-in-the-coronavirus-warren-buffett-isnt/
32. https://fortune.com/fortune500/2019/berkshire-hathaway/
33. https://threeinsurance.com/
34. https://www.orange-business.com/en/magazine/six-key-elements-of-great-customer-experience

35. https://www.qualtrics.com/blog/amazon-customer-experience-leader/
36. https://www.ameyo.com/blog/customer-experience-quotes
37. https://www.superoffice.com/blog/customer-experience-strategy/
38. https://www.fieldservicenews.com/blog/difference-good-great-customer-service
39. https://www.customerexperienceupdate.com/case-study/
40. https://hospitalitymanagementdegrees.net/features/how-apple-stores-give-their-customers-five-diamond-treatment-infographic/
41. https://fitsmallbusiness.com/customer-service-quotes/
42. https://www.forbes.com/sites/louiscolumbus/2018/03/04/10-charts-that-will-change-your-perspective-of-amazon-primes-growth/#2a2a86e83fee
43. https://publicwords.com/2009/07/23/debunking-the-debunkers-the-mehrabian-myth-explained-correctly/
44. https://www.forbes.com/sites/carolkinseygoman/2012/07/24/busting-5-body-language-myths/
45. https://www.mindtools.com/pages/article/Body_Language.htm
46. http://bodylanguageproject.com/the-only-book-on-body-language-that-everybody-needs-to-read/
47. https://www.userlike.com/en/blog/identify-customer-needs-expectations
48. https://loyaltylion.com/blog/the-four-needs-of-a-consumer
49. https://strategyn.com/outcome-driven-innovation-process/customer-needs/
50. https://www.helpguide.org/articles/relationships-communication/conflict-resolution-skills.htm
51. https://www.forbes.com/sites/rodgerdeanduncan/2018/05/04/avoid-the-blame-game-be-accountable-for-accountability/#7a09d9842b22
52. https://commsmasters.com/case-study-great-communication-makes-for-great-customer-service/
53.

54. http://www.wseas.us/e-library/conferences/2013/Chania/BAMPD/BAMPD-04.pdf
55. https://www.google.com/search?q=understanding+customer+needs+and+satisfying+them+images&newwindow=1&client=firefox-b-d&sxsrf=ALeKk01xVawgjppu2hWi2FH-irlG-_YjLA:1586074096676&tbm=isch&source=iu&ictx=1&fir=Ob_IqlKpnfI_TM%253A%252ChMapikNoWHE3VM%252C_&vet=1&usg=AI4_-kQ0QWnLOtFHDQQUnD3Hoiv2-HnF6w&sa=X&ved=2ahUKEwjYsfq46tDoAhVizDgGHWtVASsQ9QEwAHoECAkQBQ#imgrc=OA777XKVnPQsgM

THE GOLDEN KEYS FOR OUTSTANDING CUSTOMER EXPERIENCE

COMMUNICATION

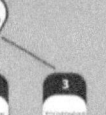

C - COMMUNICATION
U - UNDERSTANDING
S - SERVICE
T - TOLERANCE
O - OWNERSHIP
M - MANAGEMENT
E - EXPERIENCE
R - RESTORATION

SERVITUDE

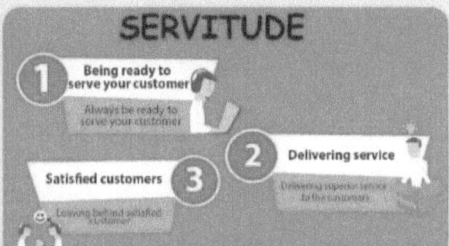

1. **Being ready to serve your customer**
Always be ready to serve your customer

2. **Delivering service**
Delivering superior service to the customer

3. **Satisfied customers**
Leaving behind satisfied customer

UNDERSTANDING

knowing what your customer needs

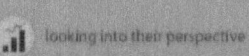
looking into their perspective

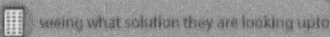
seeing what solution they are looking upto

TOLERANCE

Resolving Conflict

Managing aggressive customers through endurance

Empathy

OWNERSHIP

Taking full responsibility of an issue

The Essence Of Building Brand

Avoiding the blame game

MANAGEMENT

Then = Funnel
customer as an afterthought

Now = Flywheel
customers at the center

Marketing

Sales

EXPERIENCE

Customer Experience And Loyalty

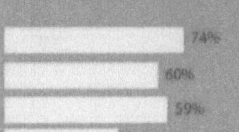

74%
60%
59%
40%

RESTORATION

AMAZON'S GROWING PRIME SUBSCRIBER

International
US

CONCLUSION

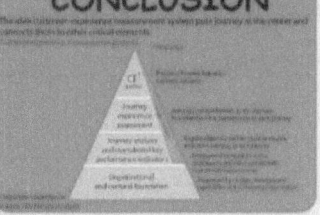